Experience

The Old Course
St Andrews Links

by *OptimizeGolf*

'This book is inspired by the land where golf
began and which continues to enchant players and
influence their game – the Old Course at
St Andrews Links. It talks of history but is grounded
in the present and looks forward to the future.
The intention is to capture and relate the unique
experience of playing the Old Course, from before
you tee off to after your round has finished,
when you are marvelling at the experience and
wondering when you will be lucky
enough to play on the hallowed turf again.'

Published by:

Personal Navigation Systems Ltd., Roseberry Court, Ellerbeck Way,
Stokesley, North Yorkshire, TS9 5QT, United Kingdom.

Printed and bound in the European Union.

ISBN: 0-9550041-1-X

Other books by *OptimizeGolf*
Experience Royal Dornoch (2005)

Bibliography
James Balfour, *Reminiscences of Golf on St Andrews Links* (1982)
Tom Jarrett, *St Andrews Golf Links–The First 600 Years* (1995)
Alister MacKenzie, *The Spirit of St Andrews (1995)*

Pictures by
Colin Palmer (Scotland Photo Library) – 8 (both)
Eric Malcolm – 9
Courtesy of the University of St Andrews – 42 (Image of ginger beer stand)
Eric Hepworth – 15, 17, 52, 82/83, 89, 94/95, 102/103, 110/111, 117
Russell Kirk – Sleeve, 11, 34, 48
Glyn Satterley – 28/29, 74/75, 116, 118/119
St Andrews Links Trust – 44/45, 119, 122/123

Text by Richard Goodale

Acknowledgements

The publishers would like to express thanks to all the contributors to this book. We are particularly grateful to Richard Goodale for his diligent research and meaningful prose. He is an experienced golfer and an accomplished golf writer.

For their stunning photography we thank Eric Hepworth and Glyn Satterley and all the photographers whose images were made available to us through the collection of St Andrews Links Trust. We also extend our thanks to Mike Woodcock and John Stewart from the Links Trust for their support and co-operation in the compilation of the book.

Contents:

Preface

The Old Course at St Andrews will always hold a special place in my heart. I fell in love with it the first time I played it in 1964, and in my five decades of travelling the globe, playing and creating golf courses, I have experienced no place like St Andrews. It has a certain mystique and a unique charm that is timeless. Some of my most memorable golf moments have been on the Old Course, punctuated by my final Open Championship in 2005. My emotions as I walked down the 18th of the Old Course for the final time and stood on the Swilcan Bridge to look back across the Links were matched only by my desire to bid a fitting farewell to an old friend. When that birdie putt fell into the hole on the final green, I felt proud that I had honoured her and the Old Course's great tradition of links golf. The memories of that final putt and of my two Open wins here will stay with me forever.

I also have warm memories of my visits to the town of St Andrews with my family. When I won the Open at the Old Course in 1970, I could sense the presence of my father, who had passed away earlier that year and who was such an instrumental part of my life and my career. My sons have caddied for me on the Old Course, and my wife and children have always been there, including greenside at the 18th hole after my final Open. They have supported me and my golf, as well as experienced the beauty and charm of the town, and the special feeling that accompanies an Open Championship at the 'Home of Golf'.

I hope that this book enhances your experiences of the Old Course, whether you have played it in the past or will in the future – or hopefully both. As it did for me, the Old Course should leave you with some wonderful memories.

Good golfing.

Jack Nicklaus

Foreword

On my first trip to Scotland, I played golf every day for three weeks, except for my second day in St Andrews. This was partly because I had been playing 36 holes a day for a week, partly because it was late April (in the days before global warming when late April in Scotland was more suitable for Commando training than for golf), and partly because I had driven from Ayrshire to the Highlands and back down to Fife. It was also a Sunday, and golf was not played on the Old Course on Sundays.

That morning, I got up late, bought a paper, read it at leisure, and then ventured out into the town for some lunch and a pint. I mingled with some students, and visited an antiquarian book shop, but all the time felt strangely attracted to the Links. So, in the cold wind and the light rain, I walked in a heavy overcoat out to and over the Old Course that I had played the day before all the way to the Eden Estuary. Here, from behind the 7th/11th green I could see all the way back to the town, and all I saw was golf. Not the golf as I knew it as an American brought up on green watered fairways surrounded by trees, but golf in its rawest form. Naturally random dunes, covered either by gorse or heavy grass or even fine fescues. Visible but indeterminate fairways and greens. Bunkers that often had to be stumbled into to be found. I wrote in my diary at the time 'savage beauty'.

Now, over 25 years later, I live within an hour's drive of the Old Course. With a family and a career, I only have the time to play it occasionally, but it never disappoints me. It is a kinder and gentler place than it was in 1978, with modern agronomic and maintenance techniques, and maybe even more beautiful when seen in the early or late light of a summer day. Beneath that beauty, however, there is still the savagery: humps and hollows that will toss your ball like a small boat on an angry sea; bunkers so insignificantly small as to be dismissed, until you find yourself in one; greens which are protected by the angles of their approaches and their massive size, even from the greatest of players.

And then, when you finish, you are back into St Andrews, one of the finest small towns in the world. Life doesn't really get much better than that.

Richard Goodale

Experiences Over Time

St Andrews is not just a beautiful town, it is one which has played, and continues to play, a significant role in Scottish, British and European history. It has been a centre of commerce, worship, learning and golf, and the latter two are still highly influential in today's global society. It is one of those places where the past meets the present and cohabits seamlessly and shamelessly.

The harbour and its trade was a major influence on the growth of the town.

The cathedral reflects the history of the town. A monument of the middle ages, it was sacked during the Reformation in 1559 and never rebuilt.

St Andrews, the town

Nature and man conspired to create the conditions which led to the birth of the game of golf in the Royal Burgh of St Andrews. Nature created the rich soil of North East Fife and the land at the confluence of the River Eden and the North Sea which allowed a harbour to be built to ship the produce from these fields to distant markets. The port and its trade brought relative prosperity, as well as products and ideas from foreign shores. The prosperity led to the town becoming both an ecclesiastical and academic centre, a cathedral city with the third oldest university in Britain, founded in 1413, after only Oxford and Cambridge.

At some point, perhaps in the 15th century, it is possible that traders from Holland brought the idea of a game which involved hitting a ball with a stick towards a distant pole. It was called 'kolven'. Folklore tells us that local shepherds, who were used to hitting rocks with their crooks whilst tending their flocks, took to this idea and adapted it to their local conditions. And yet, while the name 'golf' probably came from the Dutch, the game as we know it today undoubtedly evolved to its present form in Scotland and particularly at St Andrews. Nature provided yet another key ingredient, the linksland lying on a peninsula between the Eden Estuary and the sea.

This land had many advantages which made it an ideal place for the genesis of what we now know as 'golf'. On the one hand, from an agricultural point of view, it was 'poor' land. All that could really be grown on that sandy, saline ground were fine grasses which were suitable for little but the

St Andrews University students still undertake the 'pier walk' in term time, after chapel on Sundays.

grazing of sheep. On the other hand, those fine grasses provided minimal resistance to a rolling object. The sandy soil became compacted over time and a firm surface evolved, which promoted the quality and length of these rolls. Finally, the soil of the links drains naturally and efficiently, making the land 'playable' most of the time, even in wet seasons. And it has been known to rain in Scotland.

Two other natural factors are important to note. Firstly, the geographic location of Scotland, particularly its situation at the terminus of the Gulf Stream (Atlantic Drift), gives it a moderate climate in which outdoor sports can be played the year round. Secondly, its northern location leads to long summer nights allowing for significant play before and after normal working hours.

Despite the increasing popularity of golf in the early days, there were some conflicts in land usage. Some considered the use of the links for fun rather than archery, for example, to be abhorrent. These conflicts led to a number of bans on the game, initially by James II in 1457 and later by James III in 1471 and James IV in 1492.

However, the growth in the popularity of 'sport' reflects a profound shift in socio-economic behaviour. Young people were choosing to spend more of their increasing amount of free time having fun whacking a small ball across the linksland of Scotland, rather than practising the arts of war. Or, maybe, they were just practising those arts on a more theoretical plane.

The rights of St Andreans to play golf over St Andrews Links was established by ecclesiastical charter in 1552. James VI eventually ratified that charter in 1620, after a period of reflection, possibly due to disturbances occasioned by the Scottish Reformation such as the sack of St Andrews Cathedral in 1559. In subsequent years, the right of golfers to use the Links and have it fit for their purpose was reaffirmed.

The recorded history of golf in St Andrews from 1600 to 1750 is limited. In 1754, twenty two of the more prominent gentlemen in Fife decided to form the Society of St Andrews Golfers, to promote fraternity and the game. However, they were not the first to do so. The Honourable Company of Edinburgh Golfers, now playing at Muirfield, was founded ten years earlier, and the Royal Burgess (Edinburgh) and Royal Blackheath (London) clubs claim an even earlier genesis.

That being said, the club prospered in St Andrews and became intricately linked to the game of golf and the town. By 1834, King William IV, who was also the Duke of St Andrews, was invited to be their patron, and on his acceptance, the name of the club was changed to the Royal and Ancient Golf Club of St Andrews. At about the same time, another club, the Union Club, was also founded in St Andrews. While the older club had the history, the younger one had obtained the right to a clubhouse adjoining the Links. In 1877, after a brief courtship and a long engagement of twenty four years, the two clubs merged, retaining the name of the older club which is now affectionately known around the world as the R&A.

The Royal and Ancient Golf Club of St Andrews resides in this magnificent clubhouse.

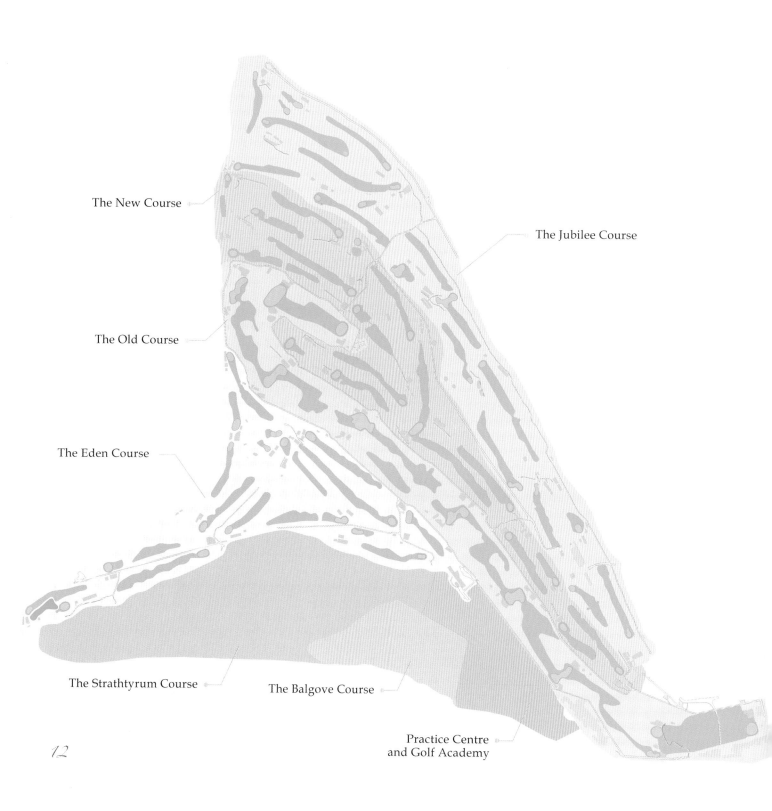

The New Course

The Jubilee Course

The Old Course

The Eden Course

The Strathtyrum Course

The Balgove Course

Practice Centre
and Golf Academy

12

St Andrews Links

By the end of the 19th century, golf had become so popular that the citizens of the town recognised a need for additional golfing facilities. The Links was acquired by the Town Council with an Act of Parliament in 1894. The New Course was built in 1895 and a short 12-hole course, the Jubilee, added in 1897. Various Acts of Parliament thereafter clarified the rights and responsibilities of the interested parties. The 1913 Act allowed for the construction of the Eden Course, designed by Harry S. Colt, of Sunningdale and Pine Valley fame, which came into play in July 1914, thus giving St Andrews four world-class links courses. In the latter part of the 20th century two new courses, the Balgove and Strathtyrum, were opened for play.

Today, golf in the town comprises of 99 holes of marvellous and varied experiences with 18 more to come in 2007/2008. The courses are all managed by the St Andrews Links Trust, created in the most recent Act of Parliament of 1974, which represents the interests of the town, the clubs and the Scottish Executive. While the Old Course remains the jewel in the crown of both St Andrews Links and the world of golf, the other courses are very worthy in their own right, and are described later in the book.

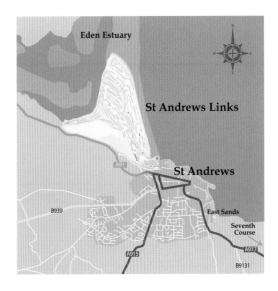

The Old Course

In the early 1800s there was no such thing as the 'Old Course'. There was just one golf course known as St Andrews Links, following much the same route as the Old Course does today, except single file, out and in, to the same set of holes, a practice which suited the relatively modest amount of play that occurred in those days.

The rest of the vast area around the St Andrews Links served primarily as nature intended, a relatively barren barrier from the sea. But even on that part of the links where golf was played, alternative uses continued into the 19th century including rabbit farming, lifeboat storage, rifle practice, clothes drying and bleaching and croquet.

However, as the fruits of the Industrial Revolution brought greater wealth and more leisure time, demand for golfing time on the Links increased. To accommodate this, improvements were made to the course during the 19th century including:

- widening the fairways and putting surfaces, by thinning out gorse

- placing two flags on each putting green, one for outward holes, another for the inward ones

- bringing the present 1st and 18th holes into play by building a dyke to staunch the tidal flow from the sea

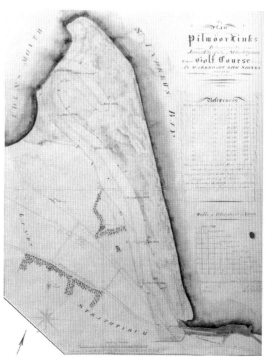

This old map shows the 280 acre area of the Links which was acquired by James Cheape from Charles and Cathcart Dempster in 1821 for an annual ground rent of £42. The purchase finally brought an end to the Rabbit Wars which had continued since the Dempsters bought the land in 1799 and introduced rabbits to the Links to provide meat and pelts. This purely commercial venture was seen to be a violation of the condition of sale by local golfers and members of the Society of St Andrews Golfers.

- building a new 18th green

- planting gorse to the expanded right (outward) side of the course to stabilise the more immature dune land in that area

The 17th green was built next to a turnpike road in the 19th century.

- reversing the play from clockwise to anti-clockwise
- building a new 17th green, including *Road* bunker, to exploit the change in direction of play

This work was done by two of the finest players in the game. First by Allan Robertson, mostly in the few years prior to his untimely death in 1859 and then by Old Tom Morris from 1865. By the 1870s, the course had evolved into very much what we see and play today but it was not until the opening of the New Course in 1895 that St Andrews Links became known as the Old Course.

About the same time, the influence of St Andrews Links began to extend far beyond the shores of North East Fife. As the oldest golfing venue, and the home of one of its most venerable and respected clubs, St Andrews became an inspiration for the growth of the game. Old Tom's reputation as both a player and keeper of the St Andrews greens, led a number of clubs to hire him to build or renovate their courses. The list of his clients in these early days is very impressive and includes Royal North Devon, Royal Dornoch, Royal County Down and Lahinch. These clubs, among others, adopted many of the general characteristics of St Andrews such as:

- having courses of 18 holes, returning to where they started rather than going point-to-point

- the use of tee boxes

- the improvement of putting surfaces, using Old Tom's theories and practices such as 'Saund, Saund and mair Saund!' and regular rolling of the greens

Old Tom's influence was further extended in the early part of the 20th century through his association with two of the most influential figures in American golf course architecture, Donald Ross and C. B. Macdonald. Ross, a Scotsman, apprenticed with Old Tom before going back to Dornoch and then off to the USA in 1899. Macdonald, an American, studied at St Andrews University from 1872 to 1875 and played golf with Morris before returning to the USA to create iconic masterpieces such as the National Golf Links. There, several holes pay tribute to the Old Course.

At about the same time, surgeon Dr Alister MacKenzie decided on a career change and became a golf course architect. He studied the Old Course extensively and applied his newly acquired knowledge to create now famous venues such as Cypress Point and Augusta National Golf Club. The latter in particular paid homage to the Old Course, with its large and wildly undulating greens, often fronted by humps and hollows, demanding the utmost respect and a full range of skills from golfers at all levels.

By the end of the 19th century, the R&A had been established as the primary rule-making body for the game, providing the sport with the stability and continuity necessary for its growth. In addition, the R&A's decision in 1919 to accept responsibility for

The Open and Amateur Championships solidified the position of St Andrews as the 'Home of Golf'.

This position has continually been strengthened in the modern era, partly through the globalisation of The Open Championship, and partly by its appearance at St Andrews every five years or so.

Nowadays, the R&A and the USGA collaborate to set the rules for golf throughout the world. The USGA, established in 1894 to take responsibility for rule making in the USA and Mexico, initially adopted the R&A rules of 1899 and since 1952 the two bodies have worked together to provide the consistency required for a global game.

Old Tom Morris

It is understandable why the Old Course has captivated and influenced many of today's leading course architects.

Today the Old Course remains a strong influence on the leading designers of golf courses. Some find it hard to pin down, although they acknowledge their debt. For example, Ken Bakst, the man behind the magnificent Friar's Head on Long Island, says: 'The Old Course influenced the design not in a conscious way, but in a subconscious way'. Kelly Blake Moran was influenced by how the course is integrated into the fabric of the town, and concludes: 'What I saw at the Old Course is on my mind at every site visit I make and every time I sit down at the drawing board'.

The incomparable Jack Nicklaus says: 'The Old Course has stimulated me as a designer on many occasions. I have surveyed things on a site, and all of a sudden have said, "Hey, that reminds me of something at St Andrews". We don't try to duplicate the feature but we do hope to recreate the look and feel, if we can. For a recent example, at the New Course at Grand Cypress in Orlando, the green contours are similar in many ways and we used the idea of double greens in several places. I would have to say that the Old Course has inspired me more than any golf course I have played. That is fact'.

Tom Doak, Jack's design partner at the greatly anticipated Sebonack course on Long Island, and the architect of highly regarded venues like Pacific Dunes in Oregon and Cape Kidnappers in New Zealand, cites features such as the large greens, the shrewdly placed hazards and the subtle contours at the fronts of the greens which magnify the difficulty of approach shots. And then, most fittingly, he says: 'Some people love the Old Course as a monument. I love it as a golf course'.

Colin Montgomerie
Second Round – 30th September 2005

Hole	1	2	3	4	5	6	7	8	9	OUT	10	11	12	13	14	15	16	17	18	IN
Yards	376	453	397	480	568	412	390	175	352	3603	380	174	348	465	618	456	423	455	357	3676
Par	4	4	4	4	5	4	4	3	4	36	4	3	4	4	5	4	4	4	4	36
Score	⑤	⑤	⑤	4	⑤	⑤	4	3	4	30	4	3	4	4	④	4	4	4	4	35

Total Yards 7279   **Par 72**   **Gross Score 65**

The Old Course record rounds

The Old Course was lengthened from 7,115 to 7,279 yards for the 2005 Open and the lowest round of the week was 65 by South Africa's David Frost, thus creating a new course record.

Colin Montgomerie equalled this feat, scoring 65 in the second round of the 2005 Dunhill Links Championship later in the year.

Colin Montgomerie achieved his record in the 2005 Dunhill Links Championship.
His round was captured, as shown above, using OptimizeGolf's GPS System.

Prior to the lengthening of the course in 2005, Brian Davis, Kevin McAlpine and Graeme McDowell all held the record of 62.

The Old Course
Hole-by-Hole Tour

This section of the book describes the tour as a five act play, with a prologue and an epilogue, beginning when you walk from the streets of the 'auld grey toon' on to the 1st tee, and ending with your return into St Andrews after you have finished golfing for the day.

The course is presented as it is played today proceeding anti-clockwise, but it used to be played in a clockwise direction. Every year St Andrews Links Trust honours this heritage by allowing the course to be played by the 'reverse' route, on or about 1st April. These events have proved that the course can stand the test of time, forwards or backwards, and that the custodians of the Links have a sense of tradition, which is essential to the game of golf...

All distances shown are in yards.

Hole 1

Burn

Your entry on to the stage

Few if any golfers arrive on the 1st tee of the Old Course without knowing what to expect. Most have seen it on TV or imagined it long before they are privileged to be there. In front of them is an expansive field with a striking vista of the North Sea and the golden West Sands to the right. Immediately behind them is the imposing and sombre clubhouse of the R&A. To the left and behind is the town, and always a number of casual and not so casual visitors. It is probably the most seamless and most poignant transition from the 'real' world to the field of play in sport.

376

376   339

Traditionally, the incoming Captain of the R&A plays himself into office with a drive off the 1st tee. The person who retrieves the ball is given a gold sovereign. Although a formal affair, it continues to inspire passion to this day, and the Captain's 'drive-in' has been adopted by clubs throughout the land. When Prince Leopold, Queen Victoria's youngest son, stood there in 1876, the crowd surged forward to within 30 yards of the tee, possibly hoping for a foozle, and probably not thinking of the consequences of a well-struck but slightly thinned shot. Fortunately, HRH managed to get his ball sufficiently airborne to avoid any carnage.

24

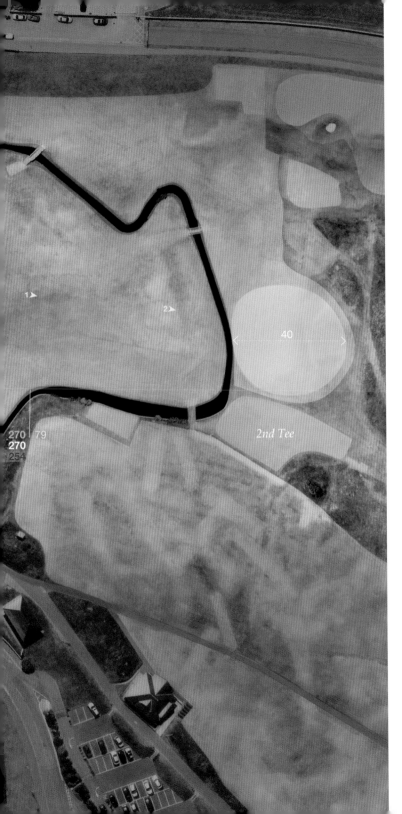

1 *Burn*

Even though the nature of this hole is fully laid out in front of you, its most fearsome hazard is felt rather than seen. The challenge is simple and straightforward, hit your tee shot to a distance from which you are most comfortable in carrying the Swilcan Burn to the green. What you see is one of the widest fairways in the world where there is plenty to aim at as long as the tee shot does not stray too far to the right. What could be more simple?

Well, there are the other four senses...

The feel of the springy turf under your feet... the fresh peaty smells of the town and the Links... the sounds of the sea and the citizens and the golfers milling around and behind you... and the dry taste in your mouth as you anticipate your adventure... and then there is the sixth sense...

1➤ *The fairway looks as wide as the Atlantic, but the Swilcan Burn*
lurks to catch the thoughtlessly long or wayward drive.

...of the eyes and souls of the people behind you, standing and watching what you are going to do with your tee shot on the most famous opening hole in the world of golf, from the same place that Tom Morris Old and Young, Vardon and Braid, Jones and Sarazen, Locke and Thomson, Palmer and Nicklaus, Ballesteros and Watson and Faldo and Woods have all stood. More than a few players standing on that tee have sensed the presence of spirits old and new.

2➤ *There is one, and only one thought in the mind of the golfer as he approaches his second shot at the 1st–*
'Get it over the burn!'

What's in a name?

Burn   The first hole takes its name from the Swilcan Burn which flows across the 1st and 18th fairways and used to form the boundary between the property of the Cheape family of Strathtyrum and the town's common.

On the 1st at the Old Course you are leaving town, but are still very much a part of it.

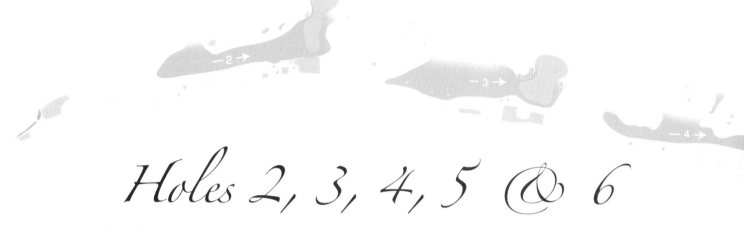

Holes 2, 3, 4, 5 & 6

Dyke, Cartgate (Out), Ginger Beer, Hole O'Cross (Out), Heathery (Out)

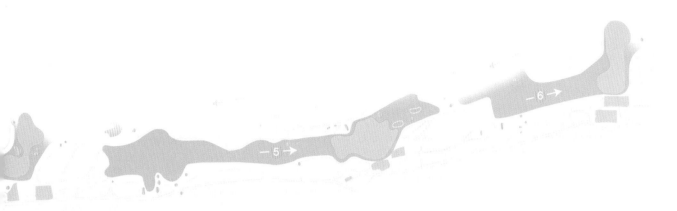

Act I

And now for something completely different…

Once you have crossed the Swilcan Burn, you enter a very different land. In front of you off the 2nd tee is broken ground, punctuated by stands of gorse, obscuring your view of the fairway ahead. In the mid-19th century it was decided to widen the course and adopt Old Daw Anderson's idea to create double greens to speed up play and increase interest in the game.

For the next five holes the player is confronted with a series of mysteries and challenges. For visitors it can be an unsettling journey. Even for the well initiated, blind shots, hidden bunkers and humps and hollows that divert balls from their line and length are always in the mind. Uncertainty is a sensation that is never conquered on the Old Course.

In 2005, with advances in technology and player skill and fitness rampant, the Championship tee for the 2nd was moved back over 40 yards, to the edge of the Ladies' Putting Green ('The Himalayas'). The tee shot from there is daunting, perhaps even matching how the hole might have played in the late 19th century from the regular tees, when golfers were using wooden clubs to strike 'gutty' balls. [1]

298
247
222 \ 140

Cheape's

241
206
171 \ 193

287
252
218 \ 148

375

411

453

The Himalayas Putting Green

32

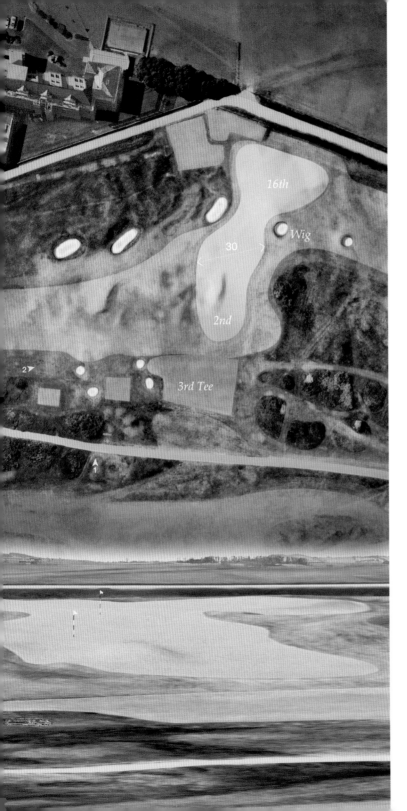

2 Dyke

The route to the green is unclear, but your caddie or experience will tell you that *Cheape's* bunker guards the generally more open left side of the fairway and a drive to the right will flirt with the whins and give you a less favourable angle to the green. Once you stride over the initial humps the essential nature of the Old Course is revealed: a fairway which heaves like the open sea; a shot to the green that demands careful thought, and not just a correct yardage.

What's in a name?

Dyke This hole shares its green with the 16th hole (*Corner of the Dyke*). The corner of the dyke is in front of the hotel, near *Cheape's* bunker.

1➤ **Left** *Looking across from beyond the tees on the 3rd.*

1. Balls moulded from the natural latex sap 'gutta percha' of certain Asian evergreen trees.

The undulating ground approaching the green makes it one of the most difficult holes on the Old Course.

2➤ *When the pin is on the left side, the humps and hollows in front of the green make it one of the most difficult to approach.*

The green itself is wide but shallow. Unless the pin is on the flattish right side, the approach must be along the ground, negotiating a crumpled ridge just in front and protecting the left half of the green. This ridge is reflected by a smaller one on the green, much as large waves are mirrored by smaller ones as they roll into shore. The diagonal nature of these ridges shows the real value of a drive up the left-hand side, as it is the only angle from which you can find a straight line to the pin. Whilst relatively short, this hole is among the more difficult on the course. Manufacturing a cunning little bump and run from 150 yards is not always in one's bag on only the second hole of the round.

The Principal's Nose group of bunkers used to lie in the middle of the driving line off the tee, at the perfect distance to catch a good drive with the old gutty ball.

Principal's Nose

244 134
215
164

3

267 106
240
191

1

321

370

397

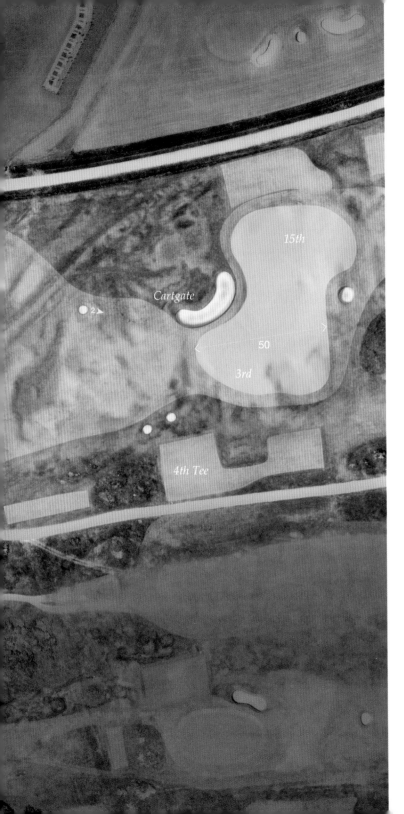

3 Cartgate (Out)

■ 397 □ 370 ■ 321 • Par 4

Once again you have a blind tee shot, and again there is a double green pinched in at the centre-left by a bunker. To the novice, this may just seem a repeat of the second hole, but with experience and further study the personality of this hole will reveal itself. It is shorter, and seemingly narrower from the tee than its predecessor, but there is substantial unseen room to the left once the rough ground is cleared. That said, the ridge in front of the green is slightly steeper, and the dip behind slightly deeper, so the demands of both the drive and the second shot are more intense.

The drive should ideally be down the right side of the fairway, skirting the gorse but missing the seemingly randomly placed pot bunkers. From here the second is a little easier having taken Cartgate bunker out of play.

The green is huge and wildly contoured, particularly at the back right, so knowing the day's pin position can be crucial.

1➤ *An unusual view of the 3rd hole from above the main tee. Even from here the pot bunkers on the right are difficult to see.*

What's in a name?

Cartgate Another hole with a shared green and a shared name, so named because of its close proximity to an old cart track that crossed the fairway. Traces of the track can still be seen on the picture on the previous page.

2➤ *If you've driven to the left of the fairway Cartgate bunker features largely in the approach to the green.*

3➤ *The approach from the right opens up the green almost taking Cartgate bunker out of play.*

Many locals deliberately drive down the right side of the path onto the 2nd of the New Course. From here the approach to the green can be less intimidating.

Rob's

264
249 \142

Sutherland

287
220
212 \169

51

13

419   401

480

40

4 Ginger Beer

■ 480 □ 419 ■ 401 • Par 4/5

On this hole, the density of the hazard placement further intensifies. There are bunkers to the right of the narrow driving channel and the *Sutherland* and *Cottage* bunkers waiting to gather any drive hit too far left of the 'safe' line.

In effect there is a small landing area between hillocks on the left which will give you a relatively flat lie and some sight of the pin on the green. The green has similarities to the previous hole, but is shallower and narrower.

Any approach shot hit too far left will find the large bunker between the 4th and 14th greens. An approach falling short will undoubtedly be deflected by the large central mound guarding the green.

1➤ *The approach from the left side of the fairway is hazardous, with numerous bunkers and the large mound to contend with.*

What's in a name?

Ginger Beer This hole used to be known as *Cunnin' Links* because the only approach to the green was down a narrow fairway lined with gorse. This was home to innumerable rabbits, or *'cuniggis'* as they were known in old Scots. Nowadays it is known as the *Ginger Beer Hole* for it was here that Old Daw Anderson had his mobile refreshment stand dispensing ginger beer, and, if you were privy to inside information, something a little more bracing.

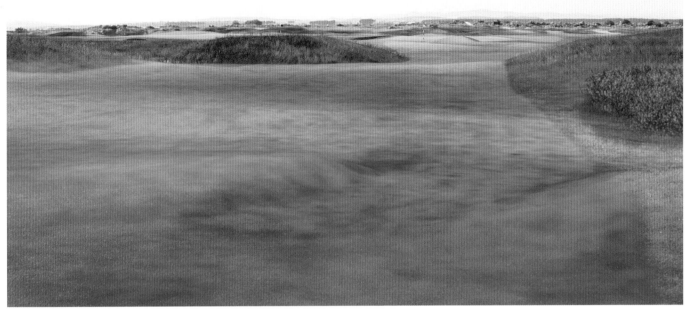

2➤ *The line in from the right side of the fairway is more direct with the only obstacle being the large mound in front of the green.*

What's in a name?

Students' bunkers A group of three bunkers so named from the practice of university students who didn't have time to play a full round. They would play four holes out and then four back.

A late summer view of the 4th green from Students' bunkers.

This is normally one of the easier holes when the Open is played on the Old Course, with a stroke average under the par of 5. For the average golfer, however, the narrowness of the fairway and the sheer number of hazards between the tee and the green can make it a nightmare. Two safe shots and a pitch would get most players home in three. However, how many can avoid the temptation of going for the green in two when the wind is favourable and the ground firm and fast.

The Elysian Fields

Beard

Benty

Hell

Kitchen

16

217
158 250

2 ›

Pulpit

258
200

566   514   454

46

5 Hole O'Cross (Out)

■ 568 □ 514 ■ 454 • Par 5

The 5th hole shares most of its space with the other, and more famous par 5 on the course, the 14th (*Long*). The objective off the tee is to avoid a cluster of bunkers on the right and then hope to carry your second shot over the ridge in which *Spectacles* bunkers sit, 30 yards or so short of the green.

However, even if you are able to do so, a massive hollow between the ridge and the green will frustrate all but the most well struck shot. Uniquely for the double greens on the course, this one stretches from front to back. Although in practice only the front half is used for the outward pin, a thinned approach could leave you with a putt of almost 100 yards.

1➤ **Left** *The 5th green from across the 14th.*

Looking towards the 5th green, you are completely unaware of the deep hollow between Spectacles bunkers and the green.

2➤ *Even with a good drive, it is a long shot to clear the ridge in which the Spectacles sit.*
The safe strategy is to lay up short, leaving an easy pitch to the green.

What's in a name?

Hole O'Cross Some say this hole took its name from the chasm which players had to cross when approaching the green. Others say that it got its name because it was the first green to have two holes cut on it, one for outgoing players and one for incoming players. Consequently they could cross on the green.

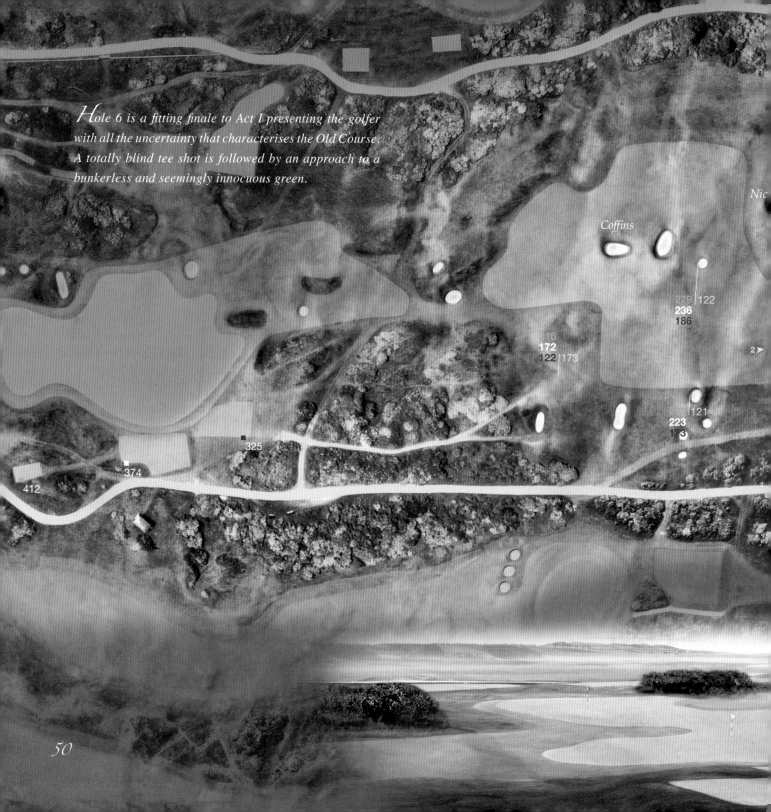

Hole 6 is a fitting finale to Act I presenting the golfer with all the uncertainty that characterises the Old Course. A totally blind tee shot is followed by an approach to a bunkerless and seemingly innocuous green.

Nic

Coffins

279 | 122
236
186

16
172
122 | 173

2▶

121

223
17

325

374

412

50

6 Heathery (Out)

■ 412 □ 374 ■ 325 • Par 4

The blind drive over a hill studded with gorse must be straight and long because the area right and left up to 240 yards from the tee is infested with pot bunkers. If you have found the fairway, the main task is to choose the appropriate shot for dealing with the dip and rise that fronts the green.

If you are playing downwind and the ground is fast and the pin at the front, a bump and run may well be the more successful option. If the pin is further back, and the wind in your face, an aerial shot will do, but with a 42 yard deep green, getting the distance right is difficult.

The tee shot is blind over gorse bushes to a fairway littered with bunkers for the first 240 yards.

The pot bunkers on the Old Course rarely offer an easy recovery to the green.

What's in a name?

Heathery Previously known as *Muir Hole, Heathery Hole* or *Hole o' Shell*. The hole featured large areas of heather and this could be where either of the first two names came from. *Hole o' Shell* came from the green which had no grass whatsoever and consisted of shells and sand which were rolled flat on top of a soft, heather covering.

2➤ *There is a gully guarding the front of the green which is difficult to see from the fairway.*
A bold bump and run will be rewarded, but a timid shot will end up nestling at the bottom of the gully.

Holes 7, 8, 9, 10, 11 & 12

High (Out), Short, End, Bobby Jones, High (In), Heathery (In)

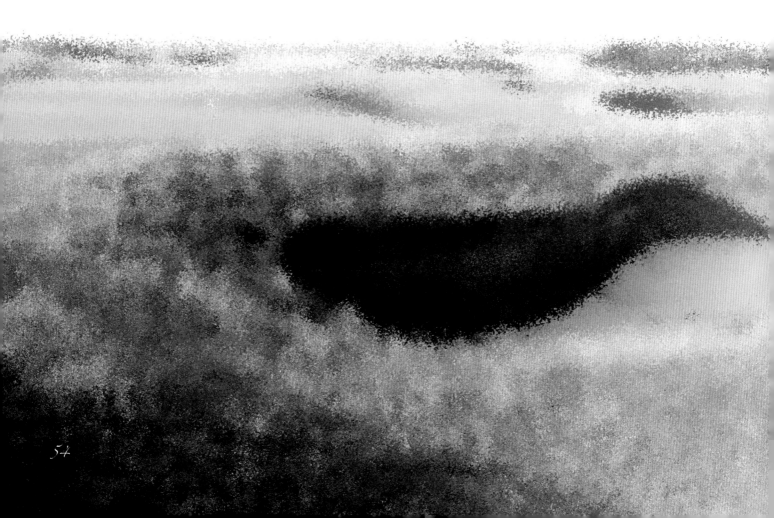

Act II

The Loop

This act begins as the quintessence of Act I with the blindest drive over the highest of the gorse, but once you climb over that hill, a celebration of golf is revealed to you. You can see and smell the water, and to the left of the green you are heading towards you can see the pin of the 11th, on the same long and narrow dune fronting the Eden Estuary. By the time you have completed the 'loop' and removed your ball from the 12th hole, you will have visited a cornucopia of short and moderate-length golfing experiences which will have either made or broken your round. Most golfers hope to be able to play these six holes better than their handicap would suggest, but, as with the rest of the Old Course, hopes are only achieved through good play and good fortune.

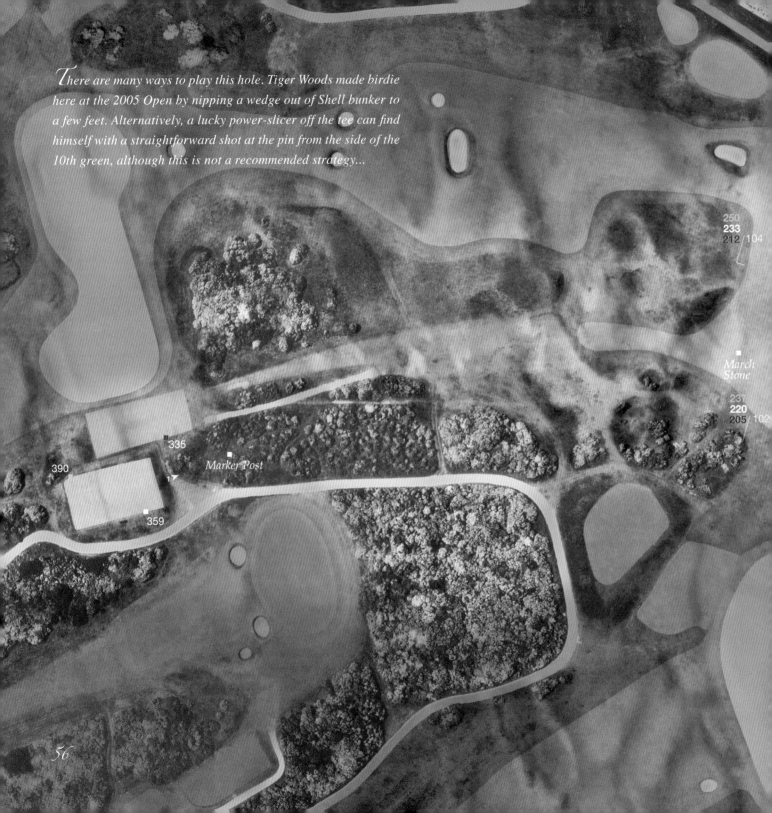

There are many ways to play this hole. Tiger Woods made birdie here at the 2005 Open by nipping a wedge out of Shell bunker to a few feet. Alternatively, a lucky power-slicer off the tee can find himself with a straightforward shot at the pin from the side of the 10th green, although this is not a recommended strategy...

250
233
212 / 104

March
Stone

237
220
205 / 102

335

390

Marker Post

359

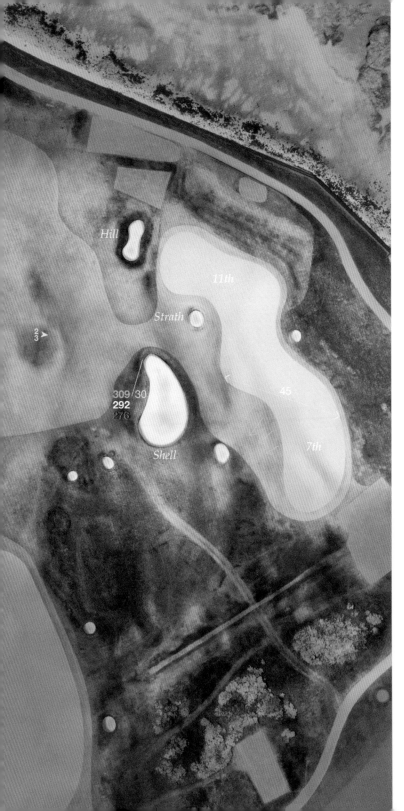

7 *High (Out)*

■ 390 ☐ 359 ■ 335 • Par 4

The bold shot is to aim straight over the marker post with a club which will take you as close to the massive *Shell* bunker as possible without going in; normally a three wood or long iron in favourable conditions, for the more proficient player. From the fairway you will probably be able to see the bottom of a pin for the first time since the opening hole. The green looks inviting with its left to right and back to front slopes which are likely to funnel well-struck shots towards most pin locations. One must, however, not be fooled by the 40 yards or so of dead ground between *Shell* bunker and the green. The number of tucks and rolls here will leave anything but a boldly played shot short.

What's in a name?

High   So named because of the commanding position of its green overlooking the Eden Estuary.

Shell bunker   This massive bunker was known as *Cockle Shell* because of its base of cockle shells which have long since disappeared under the sand.

1➤ *The tiger line for the tee shot is over the middle of the gorse. However, a less intimidating option is to aim left of the gorse to open fairway but this leaves a longer and more difficult approach along the length of the green.*

2➤ *When you arrive at your ball and look at your next shot do not be fooled into thinking that you only have to carry Shell bunker to reach the green.*

3➤ *There is approximately 40 yards between Shell and the right half of the green.*

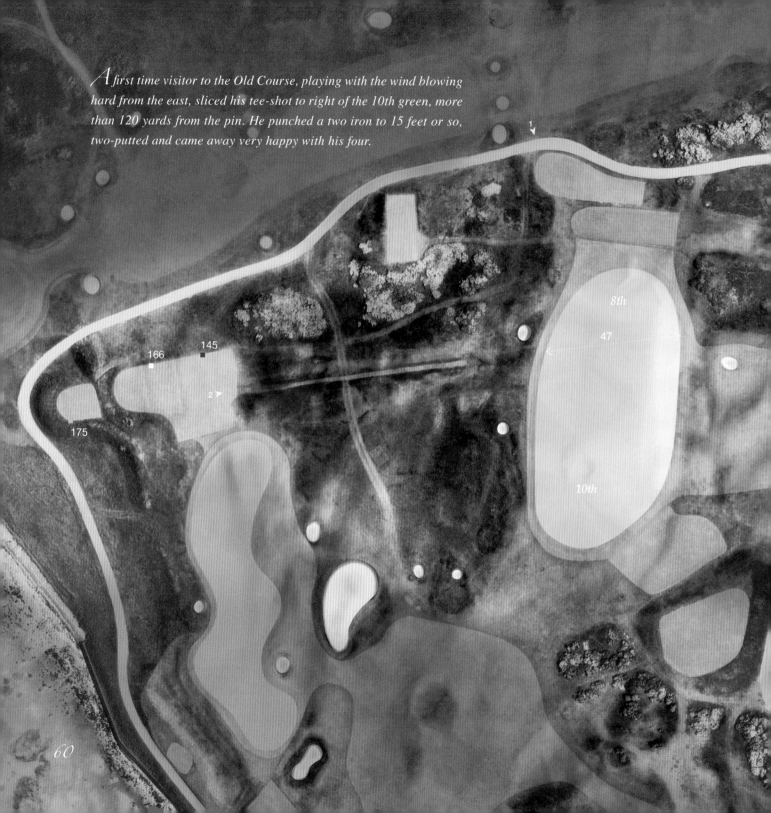

A first time visitor to the Old Course, playing with the wind blowing hard from the east, sliced his tee-shot to right of the 10th green, more than 120 yards from the pin. He punched a two iron to 15 feet or so, two-putted and came away very happy with his four.

1

8th

47

166

145

2

175

10th

8 *Short*

■ 175 □ 166 ■ 145 • Par 3

The 8th marks a shift in direction, heading back towards the town. The first of only two par 3 holes on the course, it appears straightforward with a large and relatively flat green guarded primarily by a little ridge at the front with a bunker in its face. When the pin is in the middle, this hole can be birdied, but when the pin is in the front or back, even a par can be difficult. With the pin at the front the only way of getting the ball close is to bump it in off a hillock to the right of the bunker, but that is a shot which will test the very best. When the pin is back left, it is guarded by a small hump in the green and anything long leaves a very difficult chip back.

Overall it appears to be a simple hole, but one whose subtleties defend it from all but the extremely well played shot.

1 ▶ An easy hole? A birdie opportunity? Not at all.
This hole has proved very difficult over the years, even for the pros, and demands the utmost respect.

2► *The green looks deceptively flat, because of the immense width, but it has some subtle humps and dips which can prove difficult depending on the pin position.*

During the 2005 Open, a number of the leaders found themselves in or near the gorse to the left of the 9th green after attempting to drive it from the tee. More than a few fives were recorded this way, and on a seemingly 'easy' hole. Such is the power of temptation...

Mrs Kruger

347

1 ➤

261

Kruger

2 ➤

352

64

Boase's

End Hole

39

9th

10th Tee

9 End

■ 352 □ 347 ■ 261 • Par 4

This is the simplest hole on the course. From the back tee the hole is only 352 yards and the path to the green guarded by only two centre-line bunkers 220–240 yards from the tee. The green is flat and unguarded, except for the small bunker tucked into the gorse on the left. The apparent simplicity and short length of the hole tempts so many into getting the driver out of the bag. The subtleties of the hole then reveal themselves. The gorse and the hidden bunker to the left and the open ground punctuated with gorse and bunkers to the right will catch any wayward drive.

A significant part of the fascination of golf is the juxtaposition of anticipation and reality. Just as a birdie on a difficult hole can thrill you and give you confidence, a bogey on an 'easy' one can upset your equilibrium. Holes like the 9th are a refreshing reminder of both the value of simplicity and the realisation that imperfections can enhance otherwise perfect objects. Today, golf course architects seem hellbent on creating venues consisting of 18 'classic' or 'signature' holes. The 9th at the Old Course proves the folly of this idea.

1➤ *If your tee shot lands close to Boase's and End Hole bunkers your second shot should not pose any problems.*
A bump and run, or even a long putt, should get you on to this single flat green.

2➤ *A tee shot aimed short and left of the fairway bunkers should lead to a par,
but with the green so near, why not venture the driver?*

What's in a name?

End   This was where the outward half ended and
players turned to play the same holes back again.

Kruger bunker   Three new bunkers were created by
Old Tom Morris at the time of the Boer War (1899 - 1902).
A set of two were named *Kruger* after Paul Kruger,
the President of the Transvaal, and the third one was
named *Mrs Kruger* after his wife.

The 10th green can feel like Piccadilly Circus during the rush hour. You can see people playing the 9th, 8th, 7th and the 11th holes. Whilst putting you might even find yourself sharing your space with players who have sliced from the 7th or 8th tees.

296

340

380

End Hole

Boase's

Mrs Kruger

68

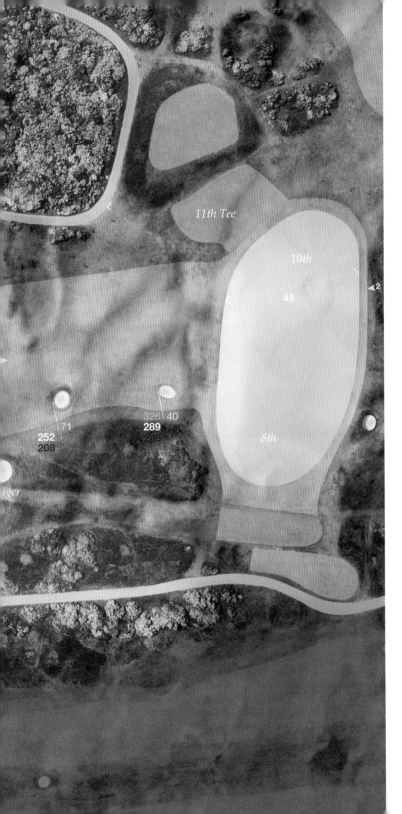

11th Tee

10th

2

48

326 40

71

289

252
208

8th

iger

10 *Bobby Jones*

■ 380 □ 340 ■ 296 • Par 4

The 10th turns back towards the Eden and its tee and the 9th green form the end of the 'shepherd's crook' that symbolises the shape of the Old Course. At first glance, this hole may look very similar to its predecessor, a short, straightforward par 4 to a seemingly simple green. The 9th and 10th share a fairway and even some hazards for shorter hitters. Nevertheless, with the change of direction, the 10th green is surrounded by crumpled ground and an approach that is much more complex than on the previous hole. In addition, the part of the double green belonging to this hole is diagonally bisected by a sharp ridge which can deflect approach shots and make long putts hard to get down in two.

What's in a name?

Bobby Jones For many years this was the only hole without a name. In 1972 it became known as *Bobby Jones* in memory of the man who was idolised at St Andrews because of his successes there and his love for the course and the people of the town. Following his death in 1971 the Town Council agreed to name the hole in his memory.

1➤ *The crumpled ground in front of the 10th green.*

2➤ *A variety of subtle slopes and planes make putting on this green a challenge.*

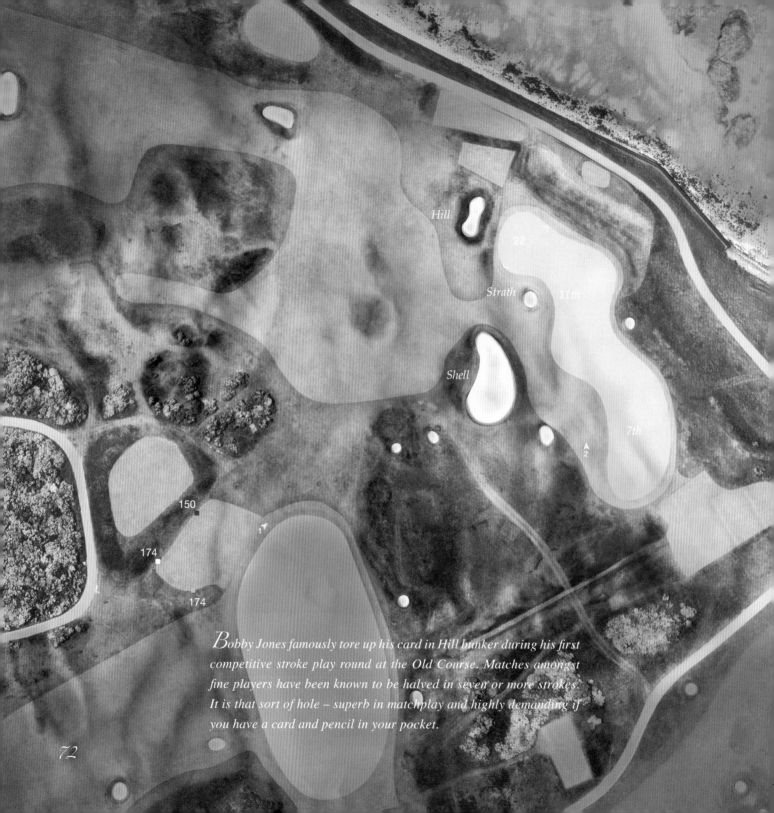

Hill

22

Strath

11th

Shell

7th

2

150

174

174

Bobby Jones famously tore up his card in Hill bunker during his first competitive stroke play round at the Old Course. Matches amongst fine players have been known to be halved in seven or more strokes. It is that sort of hole – superb in matchplay and highly demanding if you have a card and pencil in your pocket.

72

11 High (In)

■ 174 □ 174 ■ 150 • Par 3

The second and final short hole on the course, the 11th is one whose principles have been copied throughout the world of golf. A green, with its great width and receptive back to front slope, that cries out to be hit. Bunkers both short and long of the green not only make the selection of the club and the execution of the shot critical, but will also play on the mind of the less than fully confident golfer. The green has a putting surface whose slopes take back in speed what it has given you in receptiveness. Sitting on the edge of dunes fronting the Eden Estuary, the 11th is exposed to the elements as much as any hole on the course. This adds to the thrill of the challenge.

The hole can be played safely, by laying up short left to the area between the *Hill* and *Strath* bunkers. From there, a simple chip or a putt can

get one reasonably close to any pin position. Alister MacKenzie even suggested that the hole could be played entirely with a putter, and this is true, but would anyone forsake the thrill of trying to fly their ball on to that green?

To top it off, the panoramic view from the hillock on which the upper tee stands is one of the finest in golf.

What's in a name?

Strath bunker This well-known hazard honours the Strath brothers, in particular Davie, who frequently played with Tom Morris in the early 1870s.

The front of the green is guarded by perilously steep run offs as well as Strath and Shell bunkers.

1➤ *The only safe shot is between Strath and Shell bunkers.*

2➤ *The green slopes sharply from back to front but beware, an over hit downhill putt can easily be swallowed up by Strath.*

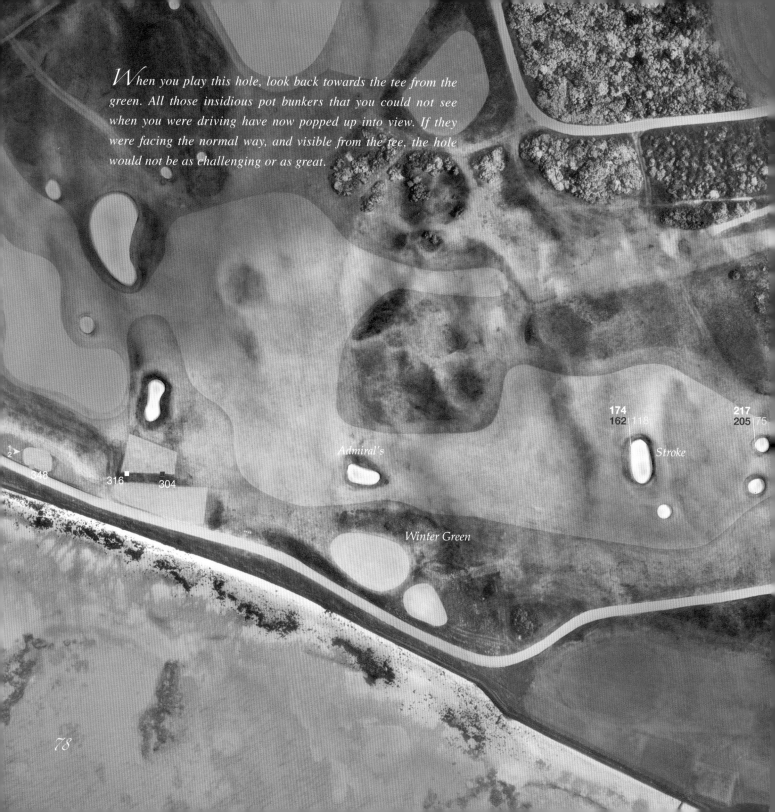

When you play this hole, look back towards the tee from the green. All those insidious pot bunkers that you could not see when you were driving have now popped up into view. If they were facing the normal way, and visible from the tee, the hole would not be as challenging or as great.

Admiral's

Winter Green

174
162 118

217
205 75

Stroke

1
2

348

316 304

78

6th

274
262 | 19

37

12th

3

12 Heathery (In)

■ 348 □ 316 ■ 304 • Par 4

The 12th constitutes the end of the Loop and like all the transition holes, it has characteristics of the land it is leaving as well as that it is moving towards. The fairway looks gently rolling, as with previous holes, and bunker-free, but that is an illusion. In fact, it is littered with bunkers that face away from the tee, harking back to before the course was widened, when this land formed the fairway of the 7th hole heading the other way.

A cluster of traps at 170-220 yards will catch many a drive off the white tee, while a solitary pot bunker 19 yards short of the green makes the players who wish to drive the putting surface think about the risks of that strategy. The green itself has a central tier running across it. When the pin is on this central tier, as it usually is for important tournaments, players have to choose between hitting a perfect wedge that will spin and hold, or running a low shot through the front level of the green and hoping it will not run too far down and off the back. When this does happen, the return chip can be as difficult as the original approach.

1➤ *The view from the tee is misleading. You may think that a straight shot*
avoiding the gorse to the left and right will not find too much trouble...

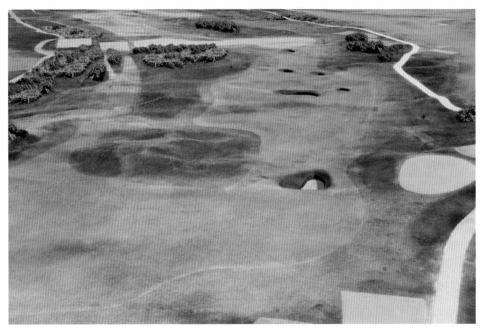

2➤ *...but if you could hover 100 feet above the tee you would see that the fairway*
is laden with bunkers which slope away from the tee.

3➤ *From the side, you can see the lateral ridge bisecting the green.*

The first time one encounters this hole it might seem ridiculously easy or cruelly unfair. After many attempts you may learn that to play it well you need to plan and execute a precise strategy of attack. But which strategy?

The 12th epitomises what golf is all about, a game of choices. A chosen strategy properly executed can be exhilarating or, when poorly executed, deflating.

Looking back towards the tee, the genius of the 12th is revealed.

Holes 13, 14, 15 & 16

Hole O'Cross (In), Long, Cartgate (In), Corner of the Dyke

Act III

The next four holes take you back to the themes explored in Act I (holes 2 – 6), which is not surprising, considering their fairways and greens were shared in the days when the course was played single file: drives toward indeterminate gorse-lined fairways dotted with pot bunkers, blind second shots to greens guarded mostly by dips and ridges at the front and greens which heave as if fluffed up by the rain and the wind.

This land is also the least changed since the earliest days of golf in St Andrews. The original course played out and back over this narrow strip, and each fairway has hazards designed for play in either direction. For example, *Hell* bunker served to torment players on both the 5th and 14th before two holes were cut in each green in 1856. There are fewer blind shots on this part of the course, but as the broad ridges on which the double greens are built slope significantly towards the sea, the greens themselves are more formidably protected. Any score which has been built on a mastery of the Loop can easily be squandered on these four holes.

The 13th contains some of the more strikingly named bunkers on the Old Course. In addition to the famed 'Coffins', there is 'Cat's Trap', the 'Lion's Mouth' and 'Walkinshaw' and all can come into play. One wonders if Mr Walkinshaw looks down kindly on this hole, despite the tribulation it must have given him in his day.

342
292
257
Cat's Trap

234
199 | 153

The Coffins

2 ▶

Walkinshaw

Nick's

1 ▶

180

207
172

465

418

377   OB

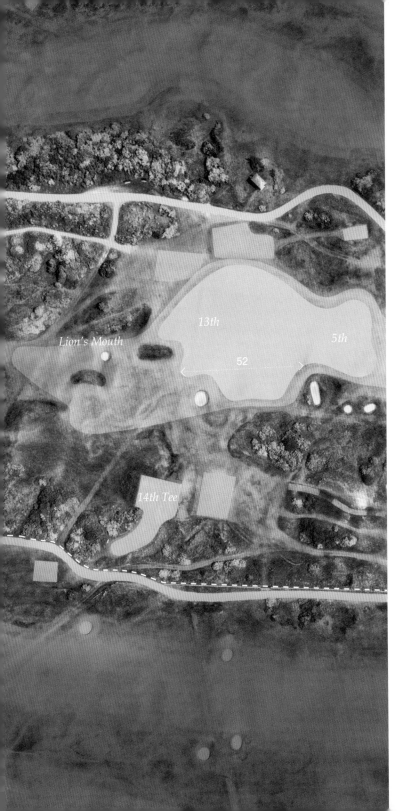

13 _Hole O'Cross (In)_

■465 □418 ■377 • Par 4/5

The 13th hole plays onto flat ground which stops abruptly at 300 yards or so out, where you are confronted with a wide transverse ridge between you and the green. Getting to that position means avoiding the _Coffins_ which are in the centre of the fairway.

A drive that flys the _Coffins_ will lie on the left side of the approach, giving players at least a glimpse of the pin. A tee shot driven to the right of the _Coffins_ will leave a blind second shot over the ridge to a green protected by broken ground in front, gorse banks on the left and two immense bunkers on the right.

Approach shots should be pitched onto the green, as it is almost impossible to play a run-up shot and expect it to roll straight to the target. The added difficulty is that the green slopes away from you and if the wind is behind then the ball can bound on, making it difficult to get close to a pin in the front third of the green.

This is a challenging hole that plays as one of the hardest relative to par when The Open is at St Andrews.

1► *The driving area is to either side of the Coffin bunkers. But if you go too far right you face a blind shot over a ridge of rough ground.*

2► *Your approach shot has to carry the extensive area of uneven ground to reach the green.*

What's in a name?

Walkinshaw bunker Mr James Walkinshaw, an enthusiastic but average golfer, frequently landed in this bunker. It was also known as *Walkinshaw's Grave* because of his regular forays there.

Nick's bunker Believed to derive from Auld Nick, a Scottish term for the Devil.

Cat's Trap bunker So called because it is unseen from the fairway and can catch your ball, much like a cat ambushes a mouse.

A fine example of a bunker at the Old Course that is integrated into the apron of the green.

165
45
124 / 344

17

530

487

618

OB

The Beardies

The Elysian Fields

Benty

As defending Open Champion in 1933, Gene Sarazen took three shots to escape from Hell bunker in the final round to lose any chance of retaining his title, and his painful experience has been felt by many other great players over the years. Since those times the banks of this famous hazard have been shored up and the edges given a clean shave, but it still demands respect even from the finest players.

14 *Long*

■ 618 ▫ 530 ■ 487 • Par 5

The name of this hole can hardly be questioned, particularly from the new championship tee which stretches it to 618 yards. Even from the front tees, the 14th can play very long, particularly if you find any of the numerous hazards whilst plotting your way up the hole.

The challenges facing you come in stages. Firstly, you must negotiate a drive past the *Beardies* down the left, and the out of bounds (Eden Course) to the right. This strip of land is called the *Elysian Fields*, the place where the Ancient Greeks believed the most worthy would go to rest after death. In one sense this is appropriate, because reaching this area can be a heavenly respite, but less so given that you must confront *Hell* on your next shot. These days, many players hope to carry *Hell* bunker, but if not, the best approach to the green is from the 5th fairway on the left. From there you have a relatively short pitch, but the front to back slope of the putting surface makes getting your shot close to the pin difficult. Most birdies on this hole come from two bold strikes, then a well-judged and executed chip and a putt.

1➤ *The ideal position from the tee is on the Elysian Fields, between the Beardies to the left and out of bounds to the right.*

2➤ *The significance of Hell bunker depends on the length of your drive. If it is long, the carry is not daunting, if short, aim left down the 5th fairway.*

3➤ *The line in from the 5th fairway provides the best approach to the green. From here you have a fairly short pitch shot in over Grave bunker.*

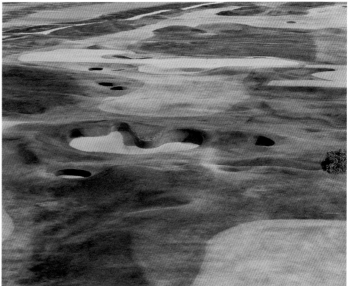

4➤ *Even laying up short of Hell has its problems.*

5➤ *Many locals will tell you that the approach to the 14th is the most challenging on the Old Course.*

What's in a name?

Long Another 'tell it like it is' name for the longest hole on the course.

Hell bunker One of the most famous bunkers on the course which has a frighteningly steep face and measures some 25 yards across.

Kitchen bunker Formerly known as *Devil's Kitchen* bunker, so named because of its original coffin-like shape.

Grave bunker Another small pot bunker whose name also derives from its original coffin shape.

Beardies bunker These four hazards took their name from the long marram grass which hung down the steep face of the bunkers and resembled beards. They may have influenced Dr Alister MacKenzie, the architect of Augusta National, who used this feature to give definition to some of the bunkers on courses he created.

*To those trapped in it, Hell bunker may seem more like something from
Dante's Inferno than a mere hazard on a golf course.*

230

192

150 210

Cottage

Sutherland

299 130

261

210

299 130

414

369

456

OB

*The Old Course immortalises many people. Two humps on this hole
give honour to a Miss Grainger. Ask your caddie to explain.*

96

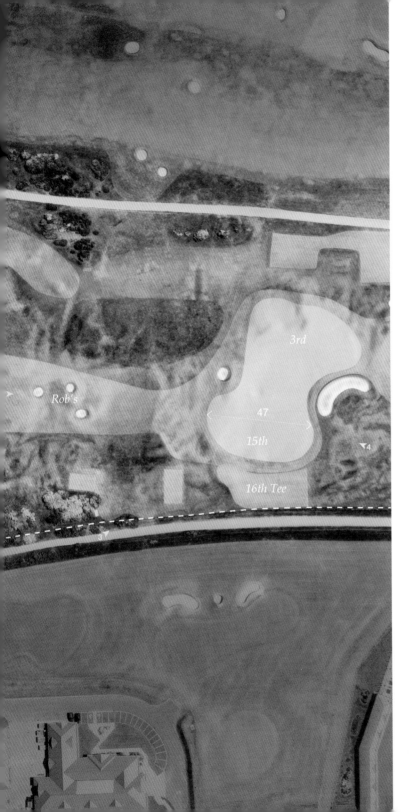

15 Cartgate (In)

■ 456 □ 414 ■ 369 • Par 4

You are now beginning to approach the town, and caddies will point you in the direction of spires and other landmarks to help guide your way. On paper, this appears to be a comparatively easy hole, at a little over 400 yards. The key to playing the hole well is the drive which should be between the two humps either side of where the fairway narrows (*Miss Grainger's Bosoms*). Failing this the second shot will be blind.

From the fairway, *Rob's* bunkers are in your line of sight for the approach shot and tend to provoke second thoughts rather than pose a real hazard.

The front of the green is protected on the left by a pot bunker and to the front and right by humps and hollows that will deflect any shot coming up short. The safe option is to take an extra club and aim for the middle of the green.

1► *Drive towards the church steeple between the two hillocks (Miss Grainger's Bosoms).*

2► *Although Rob's bunkers dominate the foreground, they should not pose a real threat.*

3➤ *The green is protected by a pot bunker and some humps and hollows which make the outcome of a bump-and-run approach very difficult to predict.*

4➤ *A shot to the centre of the green is actually the safest approach, as it will usually hold the green and raise the expectations of a birdie.*

What's in a name?

Sutherland bunker A. G. Sutherland was a rather flamboyant solicitor and keen golfer who was furious when he discovered that this bunker had been filled in on the authority of the then Green Committee. He contested their right to do so and threatened to take them to court if they didn't restore the bunker. The conflict was of great interest at the time and was a great talking point at dinner parties. On one such occasion at Strathtyrum House the guests decided to borrow shovels and toil all night to restore the bunker. Upon completion they left a note with the word Sutherland written on it. Everyone thought that this was the work of Mr Sutherland and the name has remained ever since.

Principal's
Nose

Deacon
Sime

25 147
214
159

OB

1
325

381

423

*In the 1905 Open, James Braid had a comfortable lead when
he reached the 16th in the final round. In those days, the railway
line to the right of the fairway was an integral part of the course,
and when Braid sliced his ball there, he was obliged to hit it off
the tracks. While it took him three strokes to get back onto the
grass, he still won the Championship by five shots.*

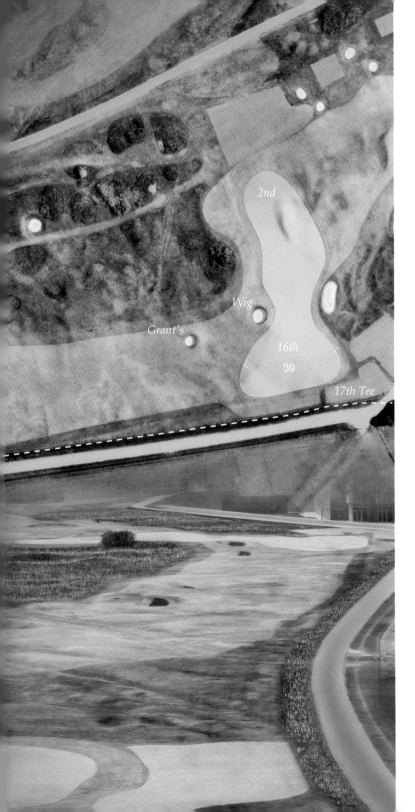

16 *Corner of the Dyke*

◼ 423 ◻ 381 ◼ 325 • Par 4

As the end of Act III approaches, the 16th encompasses all that is special about the Old Course: a rolling crumpled fairway with the boundary of the course to the right, a formidable central hazard, the *Principal's Nose* bunkers, at the normal driving distance, and then a fall-away green with an unusual shape and seemingly random contours. By the time you get to this hole, you will have become accustomed to the quirks and the charm of the course, but it still does not make it any easier or less fascinating.

There is a safe route off the tee to the left but, in recent years, the rough has been grown in to make this option less appealing. This effectively forces players to lay up before *Principal's Nose* or to try and drive down the right side and challenge the out of bounds, a line that Jack Nicklaus once called 'strictly for amateurs'.

The green is a much smaller target than most of its predecessors. It is tucked into a corner of the course next to the boundary wall and guarded by *Grant's* and *Wig* bunkers on the left. The severe slope at the front of the green will punish any approach that falls short and leave you in three-putt territory.

This pin position is one of the more challenging on the 16th green.

What's in a name?

Corner of the Dyke   Originally the second hole, this has been known as the *Corner of the Dyke* and *Balfield Hole*. The corner of the dyke is part of the old wall which bounds the Old Course Hotel and the 17th fairway. *Balfield* is an adaptation of *Ballfield* which referred to the sports field shared by two boarding schools and St Andrews University to the south of the green.

Wig bunker   In a bygone, age players had to be formally dressed to play golf. Most people wore jackets and some even wore wigs. Its full name was *Jackson's Wig*, probably to mark the captaincy of Mr E. J. Jackson in 1852.

Grant's bunker   Named after John Grant of Kilgraston, who was the R&A Club Captain in 1839 and who found himself in this bunker with annoying regularity.

Principal's Nose bunker   A group of three bunkers which resemble the nose and two nostrils. It is said that the name comes from an ugly, protruding porch on the house of the Principal of St Andrews University in South Street which was known as the *Principal's Nose*.

Hole 17

Road

Act IV

The Defining Moment

All dramas have a defining moment, or denouement, where the players are subject to a final test, the outcome of which will both define their character and determine their fate. For the Old Course, that moment comes when you stand on the 17th tee. Regardless of how well or poorly you have played up until then, what you are able to do over the next few minutes with your next few strokes will crystallise your experience.

The 17th is like nothing else on the planet. Whilst it has inspired many of the finest golf course architects in the world, it remains supreme and in itself a transition. Just as the 7th hole brings you from fields edged by gorse to the open sea, *Road* brings you from that gorse to the edge of town. You are nearly home, but face the hardest challenge on the course before getting there safely.

Cheape's

289
289
261 | 138

200
175 | 225

ŌB

455
426
455

1

2

There have been so many well documented disasters on the 17th, from Nakajima to Watson to Duval and to the entire Swedish team in one Dunhill Cup, that perhaps the most appropriate anecdote might read something like this...
MAN PARS 17TH AT FIRST ATTEMPT! 'It was just a driver, a five iron to the middle of the green and two putts,' said delighted Fred Wadsworth of Boise, Idaho.

17 *Road*

■455 · 455 ■426 • Par 4/5

The two main characteristics of this hole are as well known as any in golf: the blind drive over the sheds attached to the modern hotel (sited where the railway station once stood) and the approach to the narrow offset green bounded by a deep pot bunker and a public road. Some of the finest golfers in the world have arrived at *Road* with victory in a major tournament seemingly in hand only to be found wanting on the day. Others mastered it at the moment that defined or confirmed their greatness.

This hole epitomises the balance between the spirit of adventure and the demands for precision which define the experience of playing the Old Course. The 17th can be played boldly or cautiously with satisfaction or despair and for most players, even those of the highest echelon, both skill and luck are required to get a good result.

1➤ *When standing on the tee you realise why this is one of the most famous and most difficult holes in golf. The line to the fairway is over the dark green sheds and must carry about 180 yards to reach.*

2➤ *This is a long par 4 that was originally considered a par 5, and still plays as such for all but the finest golfers. An approach shot to the front right of the green is a good option as this leaves a short pitch down the length of this narrow but long green.*

A poorly weighted pitch, approaching from the front, can often finish on the road behind or in the famous Road bunker.

The approach to the green is fraught with danger. The steep slope at the front will deflect anything short, often into the famous *Road* bunker and an overhit approach will finish on the road or against the wall behind.

What's in a name?

Road Originally the first outward hole, it has been known as *Hole o' Hill*, *Hole o' Leslie* and the *Bridge Hole*. The *Hole o' Hill* is thought to have got its name from one of the old tees on Witch Hill. *Hole o' Leslie* may have come from Captain Thomas Leslie who was MP for the burgh from 1743 to 1761. The *Bridge Hole* took its name from the stone footbridge over the *Swilcan Burn* which is so old that its origin is a mystery.

Scholar's bunker So called because it was considered an achievement if young schoolboys could clear it with their drive when the course was played clockwise.

Cheape's bunker Named after the owners of the neighbouring Strathtyrum Estate.

3➤ *It is not unusual for players to take several attempts to escape from the Road bunker and in tournaments their torment may well be televised to the world by the camera fitted into the face of the bunker.*

This view of the green shows how narrow it is from front to back and the close proximity of the public road behind. With the pin in this position any approach shot must be played with great precision to avoid the Road bunker.

111

Hole 18

Tom Morris

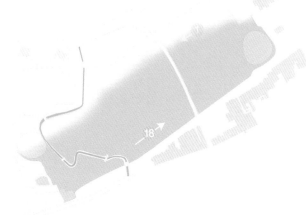

Act V

Coming home

Most plays end with the denouement, but at the Old Course there is still one act to go. As you played *Road* hole you were aware of the presence of the town, but once you stand on the final tee, you are playing into it. The view takes in the R&A clubhouse, the *Swilcan Bridge* and the 1st tee where your play began only four or so hours ago. Now, with more testing drives behind you, you are greeted again by an open field. It could not be more simple...

...or so you think.

The renowned American architect Pete Dye once said of the Tom Morris hole: '...18 is one of the best holes I've ever seen. You just can't do anything wrong on 18; you've got to birdie it every time. Only you can't'.

Swilcan Bridge

357

342

357

114

Granny
Clark's Wynd

Valley of Sin

43

18 *Tom Morris*

357 357 342 • Par 4

The final hole reflects the first with its wide open field of a fairway and its shortness, but there are differences. Now you are playing back into one of the most famous amphitheatres in world sport. There is the road and the houses on the right and there may well be players walking down the 1st to your left, and of course, there is the Swilcan Bridge and the thoughts of all the famous golfers that have crossed it.

But let us assume that you have managed to get club on ball, and now sit 100 yards or so from the green in the middle of the vast fairway. You are trying to decide how you are going to get your ball over the *Valley of Sin* to the pin. It is either a soft lob or a bump and run, but you remember Rocca and Sanders, and maybe even Old Tom Morris's words, that he built that green 'o'er the bones of dead men' (the land was once a cemetery). You know that whatever strategy you choose, finding the courage and skill to execute it when you need to may be a problem.

Then, of course, once you are on the green, you have to putt out in front of the strangers watching you from the edge of the town. It just would not seem right, on the Old Course, to offer yourself a gimme.

The morning shadows are still long as early risers complete their round.

The infamous Valley of Sin in front of the 18th green. One of the most enjoyable shots in golf must be a successful long putt across the valley and up onto this huge, sloping green in front of a gallery of onlookers.

Crossed by a burn and a public road, and heading towards the charms of the town, the 18th seamlessly melds the experiences of golf and of life as well as any venue in the world.

118

*For a day or even more, you can be Jack Nicklaus, or Arnold
Palmer, or young Tom Morris, or even a medieval shepherd
knocking a rock with his crook across St Andrews Links.*

What's in a name?

Tom Morris Named after Old Tom Morris who
constructed the green and regarded it as his finest
work. He observed it with pride from his premises in
Links Road which runs alongside the 18th fairway.

St Andrews Links Trust

St Andrews Links Trust is a charitable organisation responsible for the administration and maintenance of the golf courses at St Andrews, including the Old Course. The Trust was established in 1974 to take over the duties of the Town Council, which had been abolished following local government reform. It now employs more than 200 permanent staff and seasonal workers during the high season. The Trust manages a number of additional facilities including two clubhouses, a golf practice centre and three shops. More than 200,000 rounds are played annually over the six public courses, which feature two additional championship courses (the New and the Jubilee), two 18-hole courses (the Eden and the Strathtyrum) and a 9-hole course (the Balgove). A seventh course is currently under construction on a site south-east of St Andrews.

THE OLD COURSE
ST ANDREWS LINKS

Epilogue – The 19th Hole

You are now back where you began, and your next decision is where to reflect on your experience. You could just wander back into the town to enjoy its many and varied pleasures, or you could repair to the Links Clubhouse, or even just sit on the terrace overlooking the 1st tee and 18th green to watch those who, like you, are playing their parts on the greatest stage in golf.

Regardless of what you choose to do, you will find that the 19th hole of the Old Course at St Andrews Links is one of its finest, and like all the others will leave you with memories that you will keep with you for the rest of your life.

Hole	1	2	3	4	5	6	7	8	9	OUT	10	11	12	13	14	15	16	17	18	IN
Yards	376	453	397	480	568	412	390	175	352	**3603**	380	174	348	465	618	456	423	455	357	**3676**
SI	15	3	13	9	1	11	7	18	5		10	17	6	12	2	8	14	4	16	
Par	4	4	4	4	5	4	4	3	4	**36**	4	3	4	4	5	4	4	4	4	**36**

Total Yards 7279   Par 72

The Other St Andrews Links Courses

There are five other courses on St Andrews Links in addition to the Old Course. They are open to the public all year round and offer a true links experience to golfers of all abilities.

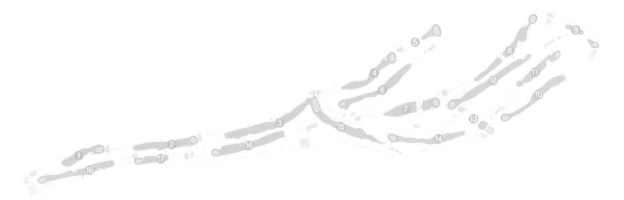

New Course

Since it opened in 1894, the New Course has been known as a worthy foil to its illustrious cousin, which lies to the left hand side of the first five of its magnificent golf holes.

The New Course will remind you of many of the challenges of the Old Course, the crumpled fairways, the seemingly omnipresent gorse, the gathering pot bunkers and the greens which roll like the sea. And yet, you learn quickly that it is a course with its own personality and character.

Jubilee Course

The Jubilee was built in 1897 by John Angus Jr for £173 3s. 8d. in only three weeks. It was formally opened for play by Mary McGregor, wife of Provost John McGregor, on 22 June 1897, which was a public holiday to mark the Diamond Jubilee of Queen Victoria. The Town Council agreed to suggestions that the course should be called the Jubilee Course. Originally designed for children and beginners, it was a very basic 12-hole course, not surprising given the cost and the speed of its construction. It was extended to 18 holes in 1905 by David Honeyman, Old Tom Morris's key assistant.

Over the next 30–40 years there was talk of improving the Jubilee, even of using much of its land to create a 'supercourse'. While this idea never came to fruition, Donald Steel remodelled and strengthened the course significantly in 1989.

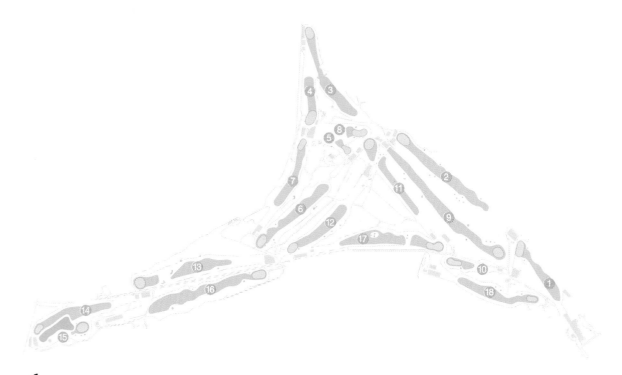

Eden Course

In the early part of the 20th century, there was increasing conflict between the town and the R&A over the rising demand for tee times. At one point, the R&A even implicitly threatened to leave St Andrews if they did not get their way. This dispute was resolved by the 1913 Act of Parliament which, among other things, required the town to build a fourth course.

This was to become the Eden, and fortunately the distinguished architect Harry S. Colt (of Sunnningdale fame and who was soon to play a

leading role in the creation of the incomparable Pine Valley) was called in to design and build the course. One of his assistants was Dr Alister MacKenzie, a surgeon just recently converted to golf course architecture who would go on to gain fame at venues such as Cypress Point, Crystal Downs and, with Bobby Jones, Augusta National Golf Club.

The course was opened on 4th July 1914 and just a few weeks later the world was at war. These days the Eden Course is extremely popular.

Strathtyrum Course

The Strathtyrum Course was opened in 1993, its name coming from the house of the nearby estate belonging to the Cheape family. As a result of the upgrading of the Jubilee Course to championship standard there was a growing need to provide an appropriate venue for the learner or casual golfer. This provided the impetus for the development of the Strathtyrum and Balgove courses.

Today, the Strathtyrum serves this function beautifully. It is a kinder, gentler course than its longer brethren, but still challenging to more adept players. At 5620 yards, long drives off the tees are not required, but accuracy is. The approaches are to greens of high quality and interest, although of less variety than the more natural greens on the other four courses at St Andrews. In homage to the Old Course, there are three double greens, each of which is cleverly designed to minimise the disruption of play and maximise player safety.

The layout allows for some sharp, but mostly subtle changes in direction. The bunkering is limited but influences player strategy and also reflects the shapes and challenges of those on the Old, the New, the Jubilee and the Eden courses. There are tremendous views as you wind your way back towards the town, and the turf is firm and springy and seems to be developing little humps and hollows as golfers walk and play over it day by day.

Balgove Course

In 1972, the Town Council bought 27 acres of farmland from the Cheape estate to build a small golf course for children and beginners.

The original design involved little more than cutting tees and greens on flat ground. In 1993, in conjunction with the building of the Strathtyrum course, the routing was changed and the greens at the Balgove were upgraded by Donald Steel to 'proper' ones, with contours, surrounding humps and hollows, and even a bunker or two. Today, the Balgove offers real golf to players just learning the game, or youngsters not big enough or strong enough to play a full-sized course, or even experienced golfers just wanting to get a few swings in for an hour or so. The nine holes range from 103 to 298 yards and all the greens require golfing skill to get near to the hole and then slot it in. It would be worthwhile for every golf complex to have a Balgove course where youngsters and beginners can learn to become more proficient in their play.

Course No 7

At the time of writing the first edition of this book, construction of a seventh course at St Andrews is well underway. Designed by the acclaimed architect David Maclay Kidd, it promises to be a spectacular cliff-top course, south-east of St Andrews, on the road to Crail. The development of another course is evidence of the willingness and ability of St Andrews Links Trust to provide new and exciting challenges to golfers worldwide.

My Experiences

You may want to record your shots and scores as a reminder
of your experience at the Old Course.

129

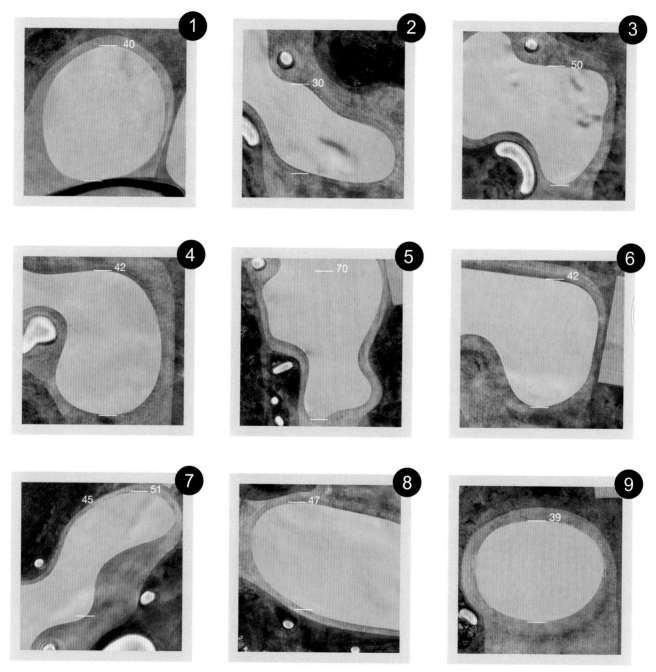

Mark your putts and pin positions on each green.

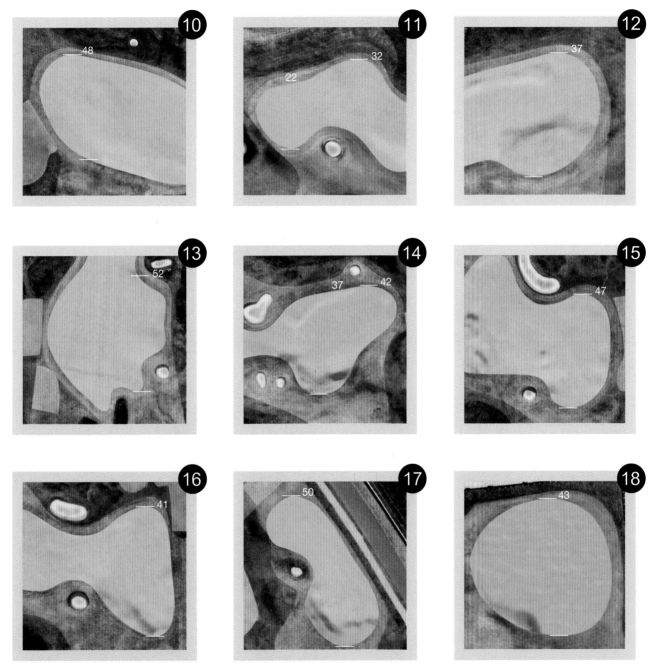

The Old Course Scorecard

Hole	Champ Yards	Medal Yards	Par	SI	Ladies Yards	Par	SI
1 Burn	376	376	4	15	339	4	12
2 Dyke	453	411	4	3	375	5	14
3 Cartgate (Out)	397	370	4	13	321	4	8
4 Ginger Beer	480	419	4	9	401	5	6
5 Hole O'Cross (Out)	568	514	5	1	454	5	2
6 Heathery (Out)	412	374	4	11	325	4	10
7 High (Out)	390	359	4	7	335	4	4
8 Short	175	166	3	18	145	3	18
9 End	352	347	4	5	261	4	16
OUT	3603	**3336**	**36**		**2956**	**38**	
10 Bobby Jones	380	340	4	10	296	4	13
11 High (In)	174	174	3	17	150	3	17
12 Heathery (In)	348	316	4	6	304	4	3
13 Hole O'Cross (In)	465	418	4	12	377	5	11
14 Long	618	530	5	2	487	5	1
15 Cartgate (In)	456	414	4	8	369	4	5
16 Corner of the Dyke	423	381	4	14	325	4	9
17 Road	455	455	4	4	426	5	7
18 Tom Morris	357	357	4	16	342	4	15
IN	3676	**3385**	**36**		**3076**	**38**	
OUT	3603	**3336**	**36**		**2956**	**38**	
TOTAL	7279	**6721**	**72**		**6032**	**76**	